LONDON BOROUGH

BUSH HILL

THE FRIENDS

by the same author

PLAYS

THE WESKER TRILOGY
(*Chicken Soup with Barley,
Roots,
I'm Talking about Jerusalem*)
THE KITCHEN
CHIPS WITH EVERYTHING
THE FOUR SEASONS
THEIR VERY OWN AND GOLDEN CITY

ESSAYS

FEARS OF FRAGMENTATION

THE FRIENDS

A Play in Two Acts
by
ARNOLD WESKER

'If the root be in confusion, nothing will be well governed'
  CONFUCIUS: 'The Great Digest'
  translated by Ezra Pound

'Now let us sleep until the world becomes morning'
  ALI MIRDREKVANDI: About General Burke and
  his men on the milky way'

JONATHAN CAPE
THIRTY BEDFORD SQUARE
LONDON

FIRST PUBLISHED 1970
© 1970 BY ARNOLD WESKER

JONATHAN CAPE LTD
30 BEDFORD SQUARE, LONDON WC1
SBN 224 61931 4

The song that appears on pp. 43–5 was written by the author and set to music (© 1969 by Wilfred Josephs) by Wilfred Josephs. Permission to use the music must be obtained from London Management, 235 Regent Street, London W1.

All performing rights of this play are fully protected, and permission to perform it, whether by amateurs or professionals, must be obtained in advance from Robin Dalton Associates, 4 Goodwin's Court, St Martin's Lane, London WC2, who can furnish all particulars.

London Borough
of Enfield
Public Libraries

H65072

822/WES

Wa 959

PRINTED IN GREAT BRITAIN
BY EBENEZER BAYLIS & SON LTD
THE TRINITY PRESS, WORCESTER, AND LONDON
BOUND BY G. & J. KITCAT LTD, LONDON

First performed by Stockholm's Stadstea at the Lilla Teatern, on January 24th, 1970, directed by Arnold Wesker, designed by Teresa Gogulska, with the following cast:

Esther	JANE SRIEDMANN
Manfred	HAKAN SERNER
Crispin	PER MYRBERG
Tessa	GURIE NORDWALL
Simone	GUN ARVIDSSON
Macey	OLOF BERGSTROM
Roland	GOSTA EKMAN

First performed in Great Britain at the Roundhouse, on May 19th, 1970, directed by Arnold Wesker, designed by Nicholas Georgiadis, with the following cast:

Esther	SUSAN ENGEL
Manfred	IAN HOLM
Crispin	ROY MARSDEN
Tessa	ANNA CROPPER
Simone	LYNN FARLEIGH
Macey	JOHN BLUTHAL
Roland	VICTOR HENRY

FOR CHARLOTTE

CHARACTERS

Esther
Manfred
Crispin
Tessa
Simone
Macey
Roland

NOTE

Confronted for the first time with directing the première of my own play, I discovered myself in a position of being able to shape the internal rhythms as I had written them. These rhythms are here indicated by the spaces in the printed text.

ACT ONE

Scene One

In a large bed, richly covered and coloured maroon, lies ESTHER. *Though ill and tired from her illness, yet she is at work slowly cutting with a pair of scissors round the shape of an enlargement of an old sepia photograph of her mother — date about 1911. This to be added to a mosaic of old photographs — some enlarged, some their original size — which she is building up on an old screen to the left of her bed. Each photograph is of a member of her family: aunts, uncles, cousins, grandparents. It is an area of the set rich in brown, black and white tones and nostalgia. Helping her is her lover* ROLAND.

MANFRED, *her brother, sits reading and writing notes by a large old carved desk.*

CRISPIN, *a friend and partner, sits restlessly at the foot of her bed, constructing his own invented toy.*

Hanging behind the bed, jarring yet touching, is a portrait of Lenin. Near the desk is a re-creation of the Crick-Watson model of the structure of the DNA molecule of heredity, two-thirds done.

All the 'Friends' are between the ages of 35 and 38.

ESTHER. Only children's faces are really beautiful. Little girls with bows and broderie anglaise; spontaneous, cruel, full of uninhibited love, like tigers. The rest is stupid and vulgar, brutal and pompous. You're not listening, Manfred.

MANFRED. I am, Ketzel, I am. Just a few more lines.

ESTHER. Except the sound of French, that's beautiful; and Russian icons and pre-Raphaelites and Venetian chandeliers.

ROLAND. Last night I slept very soundly. Long and deep.

MANFRED *(reading)*. 'The electron is a completely universal fundamental particle ...'

ROLAND. I can't remember the last time I slept so soundly.

MANFRED. '... It is stable and long-lived. For all practical purposes it is indestructible and is at present in the universe in inexhaustible numbers ...'

ESTHER. And Baroque churches and houses, fountains and market-places and the music of organs and Norman arches and wine and the cooking of friends and the sound of friends.

ROLAND. And because of that long sleep everything about me is sharp and alive.

MANFRED. 'Electron devices and electronic techniques can therefore be used as effectively in any terrestrial environment as in the near-vacuum of outer space with unrivalled speed of response and sensitivity and ...'

ESTHER. Stop it, Manfred.

MANFRED. '... can convey information more efficiently than any other kind ...'

ESTHER. It's lunacy.

MANFRED. '... and lend themselves to the control and regulation of small or large amounts of power.'

ESTHER. You surround yourself with books which you start and never finish.

ROLAND. I can't explain how beautiful that sleep was.

ESTHER. A book of essays brings you to study architecture; the book on architecture brings you to a history of cities.

ROLAND. I can isolate sounds and tastes and smells.

ESTHER. The impact of cities brings you to sociology; sociology leads you to science and electronics; and electronics involves you in trying to understand theories totally incomprehensible to you.

CRISPIN. Look at that model.

ROLAND. It was a sleep that unclogged the pores of my skin.

ACT ONE

CRISPIN. It grows, without him touching it, it grows.

ESTHER. Then he starts on another essay — and he's off again.

CRISPIN. What *is* an essay?

ESTHER. An essay on Marxist theories of art brings him to a study of the history of revolutions, which introduces him to Voltaire, who is insufficient, so he goes on to the Paris Commune which brings him back to Marx again.

CRISPIN. One man's digest of another man's thoughts. That's all an essay is.

ESTHER. And we have to listen each time he makes a leap forward to start another circle, and the room becomes cluttered with books that he buys and he buys and he buys in a great fever. That's what you've got, Manfred, a great fever.

ROLAND. Esther, lovely, don't, you'll tire yourself out.

CRISPIN. Come and sit with your sister, you callous bastard.

ESTHER. Come and sit with your sister, you callous bastard.

MANFRED (*book in hand*). Well I ask you, listen to this: '... we are moving into phases of creative disorder; everywhere the lines are blurred. Physics and biology have reached outside their classic bounds; the important work is being done within the shifting, undogmatic contours of "middle fields" such as biochemistry, molecular biology or physical chemistry ...'

CRISPIN. That model, just look at it.

MANFRED. Well, news like that terrifies me.

CRISPIN. And that model terrifies me.

ESTHER. And he grows bald and he has headaches and he refuses to wear glasses.

MANFRED. Well, doesn't it terrify you?

CRISPIN. Everything terrifies me. Babies, dogs, flies, lightning.

ESTHER. And English lawns with cats, and Italian renaissance

music and fragile, lily-like, art-nouveau girls. Beautiful!
MANFRED. ' ... we are moving into phases of creative disorder; everywhere the lines are blurred ... ' Good God!

ESTHER. Manfred, please. Can't you see I want as much of you as I can get?
MANFRED. All my life you'll have me, Kitten.
ESTHER. Will I, Manfred? In the grave, too?
MANFRED (*coming to her*). I'm a pig. I'm sorry, Ketzel. Good God, how exquisite you look, like a doll.
ESTHER. Fragile you mean, and pale – like a sick child. Oh, I get tired so quickly.
MANFRED. That wasn't quickly. You've been talking for the last two hours – a steady drone while I was reading.
CRISPIN. She used to be so silent and shy.
ESTHER. She used to have nothing to say; now she'd give long speeches if she could, in public.
CRISPIN. What would your speeches be, Ketzel?
ESTHER. Long lists of all the things I really care about, and why. Who do I hate, who do I love; what do I value, what do I despise; what pleases, what offends me? And when I knew, I'd nail the list to the door of the Commons – no, that's common – the doors of St Paul's.
MANFRED. Sleep, Ketzel, and by the time you wake you'll smell hot toast and thick coffee.
ESTHER. It's such a funny thing, sleep. A body curls itself up, closes its eyes and waits. It does absolutely nothing else, a few turns perhaps, but just lies, passively, waiting for something to happen to it.
MANFRED. Sleep. (*Kissing her*) Lovely eyes, lovely lips. No one's leaving, sleep. (*Pause. Looks at photo montage.*) Our grandfather and grandmother from Odessa. Our mother, aged nineteen. Her brothers, Theo, Nachum, Abraham.

ACT ONE

Their children, their children's children ... the cousins we've never seen ...

(*They move away from the bed.* CRISPIN *hugs himself into a red velvet wing-backed arm-chair.* ROLAND *sits on the floor in a simple Yoga position.* MANFRED *returns to his model.*)

CRISPIN (*to* ROLAND). Well that's cruel. I say that's cruel. She, your sweetheart, so ill, and you—you sit, contemplating, peacefully.
MANFRED. She's not *so* ill, Crispin. The blood-count was better yesterday.
CRISPIN. She's dying, Manfred, face it, she is.
MANFRED. We don't know that.
CRISPIN. Say it to yourself: my sister's dying.
MANFRED. We don't know—
CRISPIN. Say it to me and to Roland.
MANFRED. We don't know for certain.
ROLAND. That lunch—

—I tasted each part of it, my throat separated each part, sharply. And those smells, you know?—how meals smell just of food or a particular spice? Well this lunchtime I smelt each part. Crisply, like a sting. And sounds. It's as though I'm hearing the sound of velvet for the first time, and the movement of wood where the joints in the furniture are, and Crispin's breathing. Listen. Can't you hear the tiniest shifting of everything in the room? I think I'm turning into an aesthete.
(CRISPIN *rises suddenly, and moves to draw the curtains across the window.*)
MANFRED. But it's still daylight, you're shutting out the light.

CRISPIN. Candles. Light candles.

MANFRED. Candles? Now?

CRISPIN. There's candles, isn't there? Well, light them.

ROLAND. Pull those curtains back, Crispin, there's nothing to be frightened of.

CRISPIN. You're also frightened, you. But you won't admit it, will you?

MANFRED. Crispin!

CRISPIN. Well he is, and you — playing around with your molecules of heredity. Who the hell wants to know how the mess happened anyway?

MANFRED. Crispin, hush.

CRISPIN. Light candles, light them!

MANFRED (*hugging him*). Crispin, hush. (CRISPIN *rejects him and returns to chair alone.*) We'll light them.

(MANFRED *lights four candles sitting in candelabra. He cannot work, so they all sit in the flickering glow.*)

ROLAND. And I'm going to stop eating from now — except foods with primary tastes, like fruit and meat, very uncooked, and nuts.

CRISPIN. I'm cold.

(MANFRED *goes to the bedside and takes the cover, which he lovingly wraps around* CRISPIN.)

(*Reaching to record-player*) And music, let's have music.

MANFRED. Esther!

CRISPIN. Esther won't mind. She likes waking up to music.

(*It is the second part of Mahler's eighth symphony.*)

MANFRED. Who do I hate, who do I love; what do I value, what do I despise; what pleases, what offends me? Them's thoughts, them is.

ACT ONE

ROLAND. And I shall cease to be obese. It's so humiliating to have a body that won't do what you want it to do. I would stop using words if I could.

CRISPIN. Do you know I've stopped reading in the lavatory. I kept feeling it was an insult to the writer.

ROLAND. Funny, it's quite the reverse for me. I'm so disgusted with the act, I need a book to help me rise above it. I sometimes wish we didn't belong to this generation. Talk like that should feel, instinctively—crude.

CRISPIN. It doesn't offend.

ROLAND. Then it should. There were times when to pick our noses and put our feet on chairs and swear in front of girls and find it thrilling when they swore straight back was all delight. Such defiance, so sweet, so full of its own kind of dignity. But it's such a minor kind of dignity I feel, now; such an ephemeral delight, such a tiresome sort of defiance. There's no—no nobility in it. We're such an odious lot, us; not noble at all. No, no—majesty.

CRISPIN. Like this room. No majesty here. Dishonest, that's what it is. We own five shops selling twentieth-century interiors which we've designed, *we've* designed, mind you, and yet look at this room. Bits and pieces from other men's decades.

MANFRED. We've neglected those shops.

ROLAND. I hate them. Everything about them. I hate them.

MANFRED. Esther keeps complaining: 'Why are you here all the time? Who's looking after the shops?'

CRISPIN. Tell her. I keep saying we should tell her.

MANFRED. What good would it do, Crispin?

CRISPIN. We're going to be bankrupt. She should know.

MANFRED. She'll know soon.

CRISPIN. And why haven't the girls come?

ROLAND. Auditors are long-winded.

CRISPIN. You should have gone with them.

ROLAND. We should all have gone. Poor girls. Not even they care any longer. Only they're women, tenacious, heavy with loyalties—like unmilked cows. (*Pause*) I wonder if your eyes change colour when you turn into an aesthete?

CRISPIN. That music. Turn it off. Please!
(CRISPIN *seems to want to vanish into the arm-chair and blanket.* MANFRED *turns off the music at its most vibrantly passionate passage.*
Silence)
ROLAND. Music never could soften pain.
CRISPIN. *You* don't think she's suffering pain, do you?
ROLAND. She aches, that's all.
CRISPIN. She says she aches but we all know—
ROLAND. There's fatigue, weariness, only that.
CRISPIN. You're a fool, Roland, after all her bleeding and that bruising—you don't want to believe it.
ROLAND. When Esther suffers pain so will I, that's how I'll know—it'll come to me also; that's what being an aesthete means.
MANFRED. That's wrong, Roland. Esther wouldn't like that. You mustn't make predictions like that to yourself, not even in a joke. I know you, you make predictions then can't find reasons why you shouldn't fulfil them.
CRISPIN. Listen to his voice. How softly he speaks, still.
MANFRED. Stop talking about me as if I wasn't here.
CRISPIN. Gentle Manfred. How does he do it? Where does he find it? All that gentleness?
MANFRED. And stop pretending cruelty, Crispin. No one believes you.

*

ACT ONE

ROLAND. Do you ever think how strange, but really strange people are? There was once a man I knew, shortly after we'd opened the partnership, who asked me to arrange the inside of a large room like a grand concert hall, with pastel murals showing vistas of people arranged on seats and in boxes listening to music. And into this room he invited his friends every Sunday morning to watch him conduct gramophone records. (*Pause*) He wasn't an aesthete.

CRISPIN. I remember, when I was working on my own, a woman rang me up, at three in the morning. She'd sat all night looking at her bedroom wall. It had to be red. There and then. It had to be painted red. And I rode to her house five miles away, on a bicycle, hopefully imagining it was a ruse to get me to her bedchamber in a needful hour. But it wasn't. There on the floor, when I arrived, was a brush and a tin of red paint and I had to work, while she watched, for three hours, sitting up in bed. And after it she paid me twenty pounds. One wall. (*Pause*) Manfred says nothing. He doesn't find the world strange. Only lovely and interesting. Explanations for everybody, no evil for him. Lovely compassions and tender opinions he has.

MANFRED. Stop talking about me as if I wasn't here.

CRISPIN. You still think we love each other, don't you?

MANFRED. And don't shout at me.

CRISPIN. If only he didn't deny the existence of evil. That's what I can't bear.

ROLAND. Stop it, Crispin.

CRISPIN. Evil, evil, Manfred, chant it, lad.

ROLAND. Crispin!

CRISPIN. Evil, Manfred. They took a child from its mother, Manfred, and smashed its head against the wall. Evil!

ROLAND. Stop it or go home.

CRISPIN. A willingness to do a thing which is the opposite of goodness. A *willingness*, a love, an active willingness. Evil! Evil, evil, evil, say it, Manfred.

ROLAND. Crispin!

CRISPIN. Say it!

MANFRED. Our trouble, Crispin, us lot, the once-upon-a-time bright lads from up north, is that we've no scholarship. Bits and pieces of information, a charming earthiness, intelligence and cheek, but — not scholarship. Look at these books here. (*He picks up a pile and throws them round him.*) Renan, Taine, Kirkegaarde, Wittgenstein, Spengler, Plato, Jung, Homer, Vico, Adorno, Lukacs, Heine, Bloch — you've not heard of half of them, have you? And half of them, two-thirds, I'll never read. Do you know, new knowledge disrupts me. Because there's no solid rock of learning in this thin, undernourished brain of mine, so each fresh discovery of a fact or an idea doesn't replace, it undermines the last; it's got no measurement by which to judge itself, no perspective by which to evaluate its truth or its worth; it can take no proper place in that lovely long view of history scalloped out by bloody scholarship, because each new concern renders the last one unimportant. No bloody scholarship, us. And when I sometimes get a feeling that two people in love or one man afraid of death might be a supreme consideration, along comes this man with his 'we are moving into phases of creative disorder' and his 'everywhere the lines are blurred' and I've no defence. He sounds so right, I think, and besides — he's got scholarship. What's 'silly loving' and 'banal dying' in all that? Evil? You want me to confess to the knowledge of evil? I confess it. I say it — evil! So? And what shall I do with *that* bit of knowledge?

CRISPIN. Only a bloody Jew would discover evil with sadness instead of despair.

MANFRED (*moving to* ESTHER's *bed*). I'll never do anything

ACT ONE

right for you, Crispin. Look how she sleeps; so sweet. What the hell do I care for the dead knowledge of evil when I'm blessed with a sister as sweet as this?

(*Pause, listening*) The girls are coming.
(TESSA *and* SIMONE, *the last two of the Friends, enter with* MR MASON, 'MACEY', *aged about fifty-five, Jewish, who has been the manager of their main shop.*)

TESSA. Yes, the girls *are* coming and what's more they're hot and mad and full of war. Tell them, Macey.

MACEY. Tessa, I've told you, no alarms.

SIMONE. Not now, Tessa. (*Hangs up coats.*)

TESSA. And what are we in darkness for? Who's drawn the curtains.
(*She rushes to blow out the candles and violently draw aside the curtains.*)

MACEY. Alarms aren't necessary.

TESSA. Are you going mad! Candles!

MACEY. She doesn't listen.

TESSA. Broad daylight and you light candles.

MACEY. It's like talking to a brick wall.

TESSA. Look at them.

SIMONE. Come on, take off your shoes. Crispin, fetch a bowl of water. (*Goes to pour drinks.*)

TESSA. They sit fair, square and immovable.

MANFRED. Tessa, lower your voice—Esther.

TESSA. I'll wake her, shall I wake her?

SIMONE. All right now, Tessa.

TESSA. Shall I get her on to you? You'll listen to her, the darling's dying, you'll listen to her.

SIMONE. You've frightened them enough.

TESSA (*sitting in eighteenth-century chair and taking off her shoes*). Twenty years! Out! Like that!

THE FRIENDS

SIMONE. Roland, move off your haunches; it's tantalizing.

TESSA. And I've told them and told them, and they don't listen.

SIMONE. Macey, take a seat.

TESSA (*moving to stool by coffee table*). I hate that chair.

(SIMONE *joins her and massages her feet.*)

Tell them, Macey.

MACEY. That's not nice, Tessa, to come in straight away to a house and not say hello or ask about people. No grace, your generation.

ROLAND. Hallelujah!

SIMONE (*to* CRISPIN). Please!

MANFRED. Macey, I've a new thought for you. (*Picking up a book*)

TESSA. Macey's got something to say.

MANFRED. There's a man here says that the coming of print gave man a one-dimensional view of the world and crippled all his other perceptions.

TESSA. Let Macey tell you the news.

MANFRED. Ssh! He says 'the phonetic alphabet makes a break between eye and ear' and man has used this to change from 'the tribal to the civilized sphere' and 'since it's obvious that most civilized people are crude and numb in their perceptions' then it follows that the printing press has held back progress for five centuries and we must start all over again to unify the senses.

TESSA. Crispin, you stop them. Ouch! Gently, Simone, I've got bunions.

MANFRED. Isn't that staggering? Now I find that one thought alone upsets everything, every thing.

TESSA. Manfred, let Macey speak.

MACEY. What's so staggering about it? What staggers me more is that print has been around for the last five hundred years and not only is two-thirds of the world still illiterate,

ACT ONE

but even those who could read never did and still don't, so where's his proof? How can you be crippled by something you never engaged in? Maybe it's the other way round? Maybe they got crippled because they *didn't* read.

TESSA. I want them to know.

MACEY. Tessa, no alarms.

MANFRED. But words act like dams, he says.

MACEY. Nonsense! I've never heard such nonsense. Lovely things like words? 'Languor' — listen to it. It sounds like what it is — full of lingering and longing: 'languor!' 'Anguish', 'miasmatic', 'crackling', 'surreptitious', 'sonorous', 'asinine'. Lovely words. Dams? Gates more like, to everywhere, to every-possible-where. What else is there? Can you think of something better?

TESSA. He's like an old grandmother. You're like an old grandmother.

ROLAND. He is an old grandmother.

CRISPIN. Leave him alone, he's *my* grandmother.

MACEY. If you're listening to a man talking and you're not sure you like what he says, what helps you to be sure? He sounds right, but something nags at you. To *feel* he's wrong is not enough, you want to locate it, more precisely.

TESSA. Locate it, then; for Christ's sake locate it!

MACEY. He's attacking the world, let's say. He's critical. That's good, very good to be critical. It's a stupid, ignorant, vulgar place, he's saying. And you agree; most of the time it is. And he's saying it sadly; that makes you think he's noble. But still, something's missing, he doesn't sound quite right, if only you can find the right words for it. What are they? What will describe, as near precisely as matters, what's wrong?

TESSA. Have you ever heard a man talk so much?

MACEY. Let me talk! How can I know what I'm thinking if I

don't talk? Words, you're looking for the words. If only you can find them you'll understand. Suddenly, you know. He's critical, he's sad, but—but what? 'Dispassionate'! That's it, that's the word. And suddenly all the other words that sounded good—'critical' and 'sad'—are pushed just a little aside and a new view of him filters through. *His* sadness has nothing to do with the suffering of the world, it has to do with his image of himself. He wants you to see him being sad. That word 'dispassionate' has enabled you to suspect him of wanting to see the world as full of ignorance because, by comparison, he can then appear clever. And that leads you further; *because* you've discovered that he's dispassionate you then recognize that the details of his criticism are barren. There! another word that's come to you—'barren', and sterile; and so all that he's said is given a new perspective because you've found the one right word which gives a solid shape to what before was only an intangible feeling. Words dams? They're gates, precious, magnificent—lovely!

MANFRED. There's something wrong.

TESSA. Will you please let Macey tell you.

MANFRED. You sound right but there's something wrong. I'll think about it.

TESSA. Macey?

MACEY. All right, all right. It's a rotten business, it's my right to procrastinate. There! 'procrastinate', wonderful word—

TESSA. Macey!

MACEY. You're bankrupt! Manfred, Roland, Crispin—I think it's what you all wanted and it's happened. You're bankrupt.

CRISPIN (*moving to get the bowl of water*). Good!

TESSA. Good?

ACT ONE

CRISPIN. Yes, good!

MACEY. Good?

CRISPIN. Good! Good!

MACEY. But I don't understand you any more? Given up, is it? My lovely boys given up?

MANFRED. We're not boys any more, Macey. You've grown old with us so you haven't noticed.

MACEY. But you've gotten unhealthy, closed, incestuous. Is it a holiday you want? Go away then, all of you. I'll look after things, day and night I'll look after things, like always, I'll stay with it, Macey'll stay. Wouldn't I do that for you? Wouldn't I do anything for you?

ROLAND. Spell it out, Macey.

MACEY. You're not listening, even. Do I deserve that? I'll mortgage my house. I'll sell things, we'll all sell things. (*No response, they wait.*) Well, I've cracked each problem as it came up. I've kept my eye on the accounts, daily, there's no mess but there's no money. The sum is simple. You've neglected to order what you once knew would sell, you've not commissioned new designs like you used to, you've not done any yourselves, and so now sales don't equal bills and they've not been equalling bills for a long time. The reserve capital is eaten up; you've not listened to my warnings—except Tessa, and all she's done is design three new lines of wallpaper and matching fabrics and—that's it.

(CRISPIN *leaves.*)

Tessa wanted me to tell you because she said you wouldn't listen to her, so I've told you and so now I'm going— except I want to see my Esther.

ROLAND. Stay, Macey. It's not so bad. We're not really bankrupt. I wish we were, but unfortunately we've all got large private accounts. At least I have. It's hateful, I've always hated it, this trick of mine, knowing the feel of

23

money, but there we are, we're rich. The business will fold because we want it to, but the bills will be paid and adequate notice given to the staff. So now let's forget the shops, let's not talk about it this evening, or ever more. I'm becoming an aesthete.

MACEY. A what?

MANFRED. He's turning into an aesthete.

MACEY. He's turning into an aesthete? It's possible? He's had an operation or something?

*

(ESTHER *wakes up suddenly and irritably*.)

ESTHER. Where's my coffee?

TESSA. Esther!

ESTHER. It's never ready when I want it. You neglect me as well?

TESSA (*going to her*). Esther, hello, my kitten. The day's over. We're all home, together again. How are you now? You look so rested. Look at her, Simone, she has colour again.

ESTHER. Never mind my colour, where's my coffee and my hot toast? What are you all doing here? Macey, why are you here? Go back to work. I won't have all this idleness. I've never been able to bear idleness.

MACEY. Esther! Such shouting.

ESTHER. And my coffee — where is it?

MANFRED. Hush, Ketzel. I'll get it for you. You've woken up earlier than usual, that's all.

MACEY. What do you mean 'go back to work'? The day's over. And, if it wasn't over, I couldn't come and visit you? What's this?

ESTHER. Look, Macey, bruises. My body, full of bruises, look at me, my arms, my legs, full of pain. I'm racked with pain and you all stand around.

ROLAND. You haven't got pain, Esther.

ACT ONE

TESSA. Shut up, Roland.

ROLAND. She hasn't got any pain, she keeps saying she has and you believe her and I know she hasn't got any pain.

(CRISPIN *enters with a bowl, a jug of hot water and a towel.*)

CRISPIN. Tessa, your water.

MANFRED. I'll get your coffee and toast, Ketzel. (*Leaves.*)

MACEY. 'Ketzel'. I had a sister we used to call Ketzel: tiny kitten. She became a mathematician, very rabbinical she was. Esther, I got a story for you. A rabbi died and went to heaven and he managed to get a word in edgeways with God and he said, 'Hey, God, is it true you chose the Jews?' and God said, 'Yes,' and the rabbi said, 'Well, do me a favour and choose someone else.' Isn't that funny? Good, she laughs. It's all right then.

ESTHER (*despite laughing*). But I'm still so tired.

(ROLAND *rushes from room.*)

TESSA. Lie back then, Kitten. Here, lift a little and I'll rearrange your pillows. There, they need punching. Better? Do you want more?

SIMONE. Come on, Tessa, your water's here. It'll get cold.

(SIMONE *kisses* ESTHER *who closes her eyes and dozes again. Then she urges* TESSA *back to the chair, places her feet in the hot water and washes them.*)

CRISPIN. Come on, Macey, there's nowt left for thee nor me to do except drink.

MACEY. And why the dialect all of a sudden?

CRISPIN. So's not to see the seriousness of it.

MACEY. I didn't intend to stay. Say my little piece and go, that's what I intended.

CRISPIN. Eat with us, Macey. Tha's not done that in a long while; we're not together much longer.

MACEY. I feel uncomfortable, Crispin, and hurt. I love you

all still, but you don't take it like you used to. I'm like a father intruding on his children's privacy. You're all very strange to me in these surroundings. It's so large, this house, and full of other things. Not like the shop at all. Full of light and brightness there, but here—Old Nick lives here. It's too rich.

CRISPIN. Aye, it seems like it right now because we're all living together. Usually, though, it's only Manfred, Esther and Roland. But with Esther's dying—

MACEY. Stop that! Are you mad?

CRISPIN. With Esther being ill—we've all camped down.

MACEY. You don't leave each other alone, you've not been apart for weeks now. Is that what you want?

CRISPIN. We've been brought together, like, an' now noa one of us can bear to lose sight of t'other.

MACEY. I know, I know, that's just it. I've watched it. But it could go on for years. It's not good, Crispin. Tell them that. Tell them that it's not good.

CRISPIN. Nay. It's very good, Macey. We should've always lived like it; shared our property, confronted one another's problems—right! Good! *Wilt* tha stay?

MACEY. I don't know. I'll drink my drink and think about it.
(*Pause*)

TESSA. Crispin, come and brush my hair.

CRISPIN. Not while Simone's washing your feet I won't.

TESSA. All right, Simone, thanks, enough now.

(SIMONE, *hurt, leaves* TESSA *to soak her feet.* CRISPIN *brushes* TESSA's *long hair.*)

SIMONE. Another drink, Macey?

MACEY. Yes, I'll have that, thank you. And you'll make the dinner, won't you?

SIMONE. Yes.

ACT ONE

MACEY. Silent Simone, working for everyone.

SIMONE. That's my pleasure, Macey. Besides, even when I do talk they shut me up. My class credentials aren't acceptable, don't you know!

MACEY. Ha! Class! One day will I give them a lesson about class; such nonsense I've had to take from them all these years.

SIMONE. Such nonsense we've both had to take, eh, Macey?

MACEY. Poor Simone, you do no one thing and you do everything.

SIMONE. It's because I can do no *one* thing that I do everything. I'm very useless, Macey. Here, drink, stop questioning me, I'm embarrassed. It's easier doing things. (*She reaches to continue work on a small tapestry on stand.*)

MACEY. Then do something for me, Simone. Sell the business.

SIMONE. Sell it? Me?

MACEY. Don't let them wind it down. Find someone to buy it. You'll get a good price and I can stay with it. I'm too old for change.

SIMONE. You sell it, Macey. If you want to stay there you sell it.

MACEY. But I'm only a manager, you're a director.

SIMONE. Act on our behalf. I give you permission. We don't care.

MACEY. Extremes! Everything you do is an extreme. Megalomaniacs! I've always said that you were megalomaniacs. After one shop was a success you didn't open another *one* but another *five*! Esther never designed small tapestries, they had to be enormous, for cathedrals and board-room walls and airports. And look at all those books. Manfred doesn't buy one at a time, but whole libraries, from professors who die, desperately hoping their books will give him their cleverness. And Roland. A

27

brilliant man, brilliant! Figures were games for him. And look at him. He wants to become an aesthete! Once he wanted to be a voluptuary. From one extreme to another. Excessive. All of you. It's all mad and wrong. Six of the most talented people in the field and you're all — you're all — well I don't know what you're all doing. I don't understand it. It's not anything I understand at all.

SIMONE. The streets are filled with strange, young people, Macey. Beautiful boys and girls with long hair and colourful bits and pieces they buy from our shop. All styles — Victorian, art-nouveau, military — as though they're attracted by the pomp and circumstance of traditions they hated — like cats playing with mice before devouring them. And they want only one thing, these people. To love. It's as though they're surrounded by so much ugliness and greed that they have to spend all their time convincing themselves that other things exist. And they try to be frightened of nothing. Anyhow, whatever it is — I'm not much good at that kind of analysis — two of them came into the shop today and held out their hands. In one hand was a black handkerchief containing money, in the other hand a packet of plain biscuits. And one of them said, 'Have some money,' like that, 'Have some money,' as though he were offering me a cigarette. And do you know I was embarrassed. But I put my hand into the black handkerchief and took out two pennies, they were all pennies. 'Now have a biscuit,' the other one said. I was mesmerized but I took it, and ate it, and they watched me very closely, smiling and eager, as though waiting to see if I'd learned the lesson. Then they walked out, offering pennies and biscuits to other people. I heard one person say, 'Not today, thank you.'

MACEY. It makes me very angry.

SIMONE. Does it, Macey?

ACT ONE

MACEY. They all wear masks, they've all got comfortable poses.

SIMONE. Doesn't it find even a little, little echo in you?

MACEY. And they shift about in personalities that've got nothing to do with them, and they drag around some old cult, and they stick alien feelings on to themselves—

SIMONE. After all, they like our shops.

MACEY. —alien feelings! Like those shabby second-hand clothes. Nothing fits.

SIMONE. Nothing?

MACEY. All right, so they've got a—a sweet-natured grubbiness, but they're still susceptible to loud-mouthed culture and political fraudulence. They'll never produce anything, not this time round. Have to abandon hope this decade. An uncomfortable lot. It irritates me.

SIMONE. What's irritating about the young is that we're not.

MACEY. Possibly, possibly. I'm reaching the age where I employ a desperate charm in order to gain the attentions of all those lovely young girls whose silly little minds I despise. And the price I pay for this flattery is to listen to their flat, dull thoughts which they offer with that shrill immodest modesty, you know?—how they hide their awful conceits by trying to be humble? Terrible age, really; the age where I only want to hurt, give pain, make others suffer. A sour age.

(*Suddenly* MANFRED, *carrying a tray of coffee and toast in one hand, drags in* ROLAND *with the other.* ROLAND *is struggling to put on a shirt through which blood is seeping.* SIMONE *stifles a scream. He has been cutting his body with a razor and rubbing salt into it.*)

MANFRED. Look what I found this bloody fool doing.

(ESTHER *sits up but cannot see what has happened and* MANFRED *immediately goes to distract her. The others move in to* ROLAND.)

ROLAND (*hissing whisper*). Don't! Leave me.

ESTHER. Did I hear a scream?

ROLAND. And don't tell her anything.

SIMONE. It's nothing, Kitten. I broke a glass, a little cut.

(SIMONE *bends down pretending to pick up something.* TESSA *takes a towel and covers* ROLAND*'s shoulders. Then he comes deeper into the room and sits on a stool, tense from his self-inflicted pain.*)

ESTHER. Why is Roland in a towel? Roland—why are you in a towel?

SIMONE. He's just washed his hair.

(ROLAND *pathetically rubs his hair.*)

MANFRED. I'm sorry it took so long, Ketzel.

ESTHER. You know, there was once a doctor who discovered he had leukaemia because one day he bought a new microscope and tested it by looking at a sample of his own blood.

TESSA (*to* ROLAND). What have you done?

CRISPIN. Razor cuts, they're razor cuts.

MANFRED (*to* ESTHER). The blood-count was good last week, don't forget, so they must have found the right drug for you, my kitten.

ROLAND. Tell me she's not suffering.

TESSA. What good do you think you're doing, fool, what good?

ESTHER (*to* MANFRED). You know how *I* knew? Roland was making love to me one night and asked me, 'Where did you get those bruises from?' 'What bruises?' I asked him. 'Those ones,' he said, 'there, and there, and there and there and there.'

CRISPIN. And salt. He's rubbed them in with salt.

ACT ONE

ROLAND. Stop staring at me. Go away. She'll see you.

SIMONE. Let me sponge you.

ROLAND. Don't come near me. Please. Perhaps she won't die. Please God make it hurt more. I've never had any pain in my life, make it hurt more, it's not fair to give pain so unevenly, make it, make it.

TESSA. Fool!

(As he talks, ROLAND is rubbing himself, and thus rubbing the salt deeper into his wounds. In the petrified silence ESTHER becomes suspicious.)

ESTHER. What is it? Why is everyone standing around? I know what it is. It's depression time again. I'm dying and you want me to make it easier for you by pretending I'm not, isn't it? Come on now, we're all too clever for dramatic deceits like that. And what's more, your silence and pretending make my misery worse. Much, much worse. MACEY! I want to go on living! ROLAND! I *don't* want to die. MANFRED, SIMONE, TESSA! All of you. I-do-not-want-to-die. *(Pause)* My God, that was cruel of me, wasn't it. Oh, forgive me, everyone, don't take notice. I didn't mean to give you pain.

TESSA *(low and fierce to ROLAND)*. Fool, fool, fool.

ESTHER. Yes, I did. I did want to give pain. I should say I don't mind, make it easier for you, but I do—I do—I just do. *(Long pause)* Manfred, I want to walk. Help me.

(She rises, talking, MANFRED helping.)

Do you know anybody who was prepared to die? Despite all the suffering and the knowledge of suffering and man's inhumanity, everyone wants to go on living—for ever and ever, gloriously.

(She takes a stick and slowly circles the room, touching, remembering.)

Some people of course know that when they're old they'll become tired and ready to go; or else they grow to despise themselves so much for not being what they thought they were that they become anxious and eager to fade out. Not me, though. Just not me. I can't tell you how much I cherish everything. I know there's a lot that's obscene and ugly but it's never been too oppressive, I've always had the capacity not to be oppressed. *You* know that, don't you, Roland? In the end there's such sweetness, such joy in hidden places. I want to stay on and not miss anything. I want to stay with you, all of you, close and warm and happy. Why shouldn't I want that? And think — all those things I haven't done. Every year the world finds something new to offer me: another man makes music or carves an impossible shape out of the rocks or sings us a poem. Someone is always rising up, taking wing, and behind him he pulls the rest of us; and I want to be there, for every movement, every sound. Why should I want to die away from all that?

(ESTHER *falters*, CRISPIN *goes to her.*)

That's made me tired again, that has.

(ESTHER *returns to her bed, exhausted.*)

I keep wanting to talk and I keep getting tired. Manfred, take the pillows away.

(ESTHER *exhaustedly slides down into her bed with eyes closed.*

SIMONE *moves to* MANFRED, *who has left the bed and is desolate and cannot contain his anguish. She clasps him in her arms.*)

TESSA (*rushes to* CRISPIN). Hold me, Crispin, just this once more, I'll not ask thee again.

(*She clasps him but his response betrays some reluctance.*

MACEY, *disturbed, moves as though drawn, despite himself, to* ROLAND. *He picks up the sponge, unable to believe he could ever bring himself to do it, and gently sponges* ROLAND's *back.*)

ACT ONE

MACEY. You're children, you're all children. Go away from each other. It's not right, you don't know what you're doing, any of you.

Scene Two

Three hours have passed. Dinner has been eaten.
ESTHER *sleeps.* MANFRED *lies on top of the blankets close to her.*
SIMONE *sews buttons on a shirt.* MACEY *has remained. He is a little drunk.*

MACEY. Why don't I go? (*Pause*) There's a great stillness in you, girl. I've never known anyone to radiate such calm. How can you be still in a house like this? (*Pause*) Why don't I go?

SIMONE. Stay, Macey. There's no shop tomorrow. Help us kill Sunday.

MACEY. Look at him, Manfred, there. He won't leave her alone. He can't hold on *for* her. (*Pause*) I've drunk too much. Everyone's crawled into some corner of the house and no one's said anything to me and I don't know what I'm supposed to do. Why are you so still?

SIMONE. Everyone tells me that. It's not stillness really, it's fear. A protective silence. If I say too much or do too much I'm always afraid someone'll stamp on me. I feel so raw most of the time, such a useless human being.

MACEY. That lot'd miss you for a start. Cuddling their tempers when their arses need kicking.

SIMONE. That's just because I'm so desperate to be wanted. I'd do anything for that.

MACEY. Why don't I go? I feel like I've caught a disease.

SIMONE. They're lucky, the others. The same art college, same warm northern city, same kind of labouring fathers and tight-lipped mothers.

33

MACEY. Ha! Labouring fathers and tight-lipped mothers. I like that.
SIMONE. And they built the shops for them.
MACEY. Only they never came.
SIMONE. My lot came instead.
MACEY. Not Crispin's driver dad nor Roland's religious floor-scrubbing mum.
SIMONE. But slim young actresses and architects' wives.
MACEY. Not Tessa's bricklaying brothers.
SIMONE. But politicians' daughters.
MACEY (*indicating* MANFRED *and* ESTHER). Not even their parents: The Leeds Jewish Anarchists' Association— ten hours a day stitching linings; no furniture and all books.
SIMONE. And you know, Macey, it's broken their hearts.
MACEY. I know it.

(MANFRED *comes forward. He seems in a trance.*)
MANFRED. How strange.
MACEY. So you were awake then?
MANFRED. I think I've been dreaming.
MACEY. Oh, so you weren't awake then?
MANFRED. But I wasn't asleep.
MACEY. So you *were* awake then!
MANFRED. I've got a powerful urge to say something. As though I've been instructed, as though I've had a vision.
MACEY. Good. Now I *am* going.
MANFRED. But I can't bring myself to say it. It sounds so banal. And yet lying there, it didn't seem stupid, it seemed profound, and desperately urgent. Even now, I don't feel fully awake, I feel—don't laugh—possessed. But—(*turning to* ESTHER) possessed by her. I want to say—(*He finds it difficult.*)—I've got to say—we must be

ACT ONE

honest. That's all. Just four words. Isn't that dull? But it was a great need, all of a sudden; we—I must be honest. Who do *I* hate, who do *I* love, what do I value, what do I despise, what pleases *me*, what offends *me*? Esther's questions. And I want to go around asking everybody else. What offends *them*? That's why revolutions happen, isn't it?—something offends. Macey, you, why are you a manager?

MACEY. I should've gone.

MANFRED. You manage other men's affairs, you don't create or invent or produce but you manage what other men produce. Why? A man who loves words. Why? You won't answer, will you.

MACEY. Simone, Manfred—good night to you.

MANFRED. Esther's dying, Macey. We're growing old bit by bit. Every word is a second, passing. It'll never return, never. That's so absolute. I shall never be young again. I shall never laugh the same way again. I shall never love for the first time again, never discover my first sight of the sea, nor climb my first mountain, nor stumble across literature, never; I'll reach out to recapture or remember—but the first ecstasy of all things? Never again. So, it's important. I *must* know. What do I really love? What do I dare to say I despise? (*As though trying to remember something he once told himself secretly*) Englishmen! I despise the Englishman. His beliefs embarrass him. (*Pause*) Is that all I wanted to say? A bit weak, wasn't it? (*Trying again*) Belief demands passion and passion exposes him so he believes in nothing. He's not terrified of action. Action, battles, defeats—they're easy for him. No, it's ridicule. Passion invites ridicule; men wither from that. Listen to an Englishman talk, there's no real sweetness there, is there? No simplicity, only sneers. The love sneer, the political sneer, the religious sneer—sad. (*Pause, suddenly:*) Macey's

35

right. We must sell the shop, not fold it up. Sell it and start again, something else. I want to talk about it. Simone, call Tessa and Crispin, drag Roland out from wherever he's crawled—we'll talk, plot. It's so long since we've plotted. (*Long pause*) Terrible, isn't it? I can't bring myself to believe any of that. Lying there it sounded so logical and right; but saying it, actually using the words— nothing. Stale.

(MANFRED *returns to his model, adding to it unenthusiastically.*)

SIMONE. Manfred, can *I* say something to you—?
MANFRED. I don't think so, Simone ... Thanks, but—forget it.

SIMONE. Play me a game of chess, Macey. Keep me company.
MACEY. I must go.
SIMONE. I'm not very good, you can beat me.
MACEY. Why don't I go?
SIMONE. Here. (*Indicates eighteenth-century chair.*) This one.
MACEY. Now.
SIMONE. Beautiful chair, isn't it?
MACEY. Before the others return.
SIMONE. I know other people's pain is a net, but stay—I beg you. Look, look at the chessmen, Crispin made them, he's made the king like Don Quixote and Sancho Panza is the Queen trying to protect him.

(*They play. While they are playing*, ROLAND *enters with 'paper' burning in his fingers. He brings it to an ashtray and watches it burn.* MACEY *is incredulous when he realizes what it is.*)

MACEY. That's money!
ROLAND. Watch. (*Takes another pound note and burns it.*) Look at it. What does it make you feel?

(MACEY, *unable to control himself, stamps it out.* SIMONE),

ACT ONE

seeing MACEY *distracted, reaches for a shirt and begins sewing on buttons.*)

So? What've you saved? Does it make you feel better now? *You* should do it. Take a pound note from your wallet and burn it. Try. Look, I'll do it again. Watch.

(MACEY *is mesmerized as* ROLAND *burns another.*)

The last time I did that was in a restaurant with Esther. She cried.

MACEY. I could never do that, never.

ROLAND. You don't know, try it.

MACEY. I could never bring my hands to strike the match. Physically, I couldn't do it. I know it without even trying.

SIMONE. You're cheating, aren't you, Roland. Three pound notes? Nothing more?

ROLAND. You're right, of course. Such little gestures for big angers. Aaaah!

SIMONE. Your back?

ROLAND. Hot. Hot and throbbing. Now I feel I want to bathe in ice. If only I didn't have to move. Pain needs contemplation, it's irritating otherwise. So petty— irritation.

(ROLAND *takes up his Yoga position.*)

(TESSA *and* CRISPIN *return. He is in a vicious mood, waving a letter at* SIMONE.)

CRISPIN. Another one.

TESSA. Crispin, no!

CRISPIN. I've found another one. Wherever I go I find thy letters and thy notes waiting for me, like an ambush. In t' pockets when I reach for cigarettes, under t' pillows, on t' desk—everywhere. Tha even posts 'em to me. We live in t' same house and tha posts me letters. Tha little mad girl, thee, why dast dae't?

SIMONE. Crispin, please, I beg you.
CRISPIN. I've told thee, again and again. I've told thee but tha dastna listen. An' what in hell is't tha' doing that for? Can't I sew me own buttons? Look at her! Look at that long, ancient, Gothic face. Full of apology for belonging to her class. Do you knoa how she sees us, Macey? As working-class heroes bringing light and beauty to our mums and brothers. Stop looking so sad for me.
SIMONE. All right, I promise, never again, but no more scenes.
CRISPIN. Nay, don't run away, I'm not ower finished yet.
SIMONE. So cruel. You're so cruel and unsubtle.
CRISPIN. Listen to t'words she uses. 'Unsubtle'. What's subtlety got to do wi' anything? She misuses words and emotions like an illiterate office girl.
SIMONE. All right, I'm hurt, you've succeeded. Don't go on.
CRISPIN. Listen to this: (*reading from letter*) 'Oh my darling. Instinctively I sense a crisis in your soul.' A crisis in my soul! That's how subtle she is. 'O God I am sad with you. Do not evade my glances of concern.' How's that for a nice, fat platitude—'Do not evade my glances of concern.' And I have to read it, every day. Words pour out of her, biliously, each one killing the one before. ' ... the mundane, mediocre, timid, dreary phrases of our heart ... the dull, safe minds ... if only we could look outside and raise the level of pleasure to great stimulation and beauty and progress and satisfaction ... ' What does any of it mean? Where dast find time to write all this great nonsense? 'Oh my dearest, what the hell does friendship mean? One feels all the depths of pain and difficulty—and you chose to insult and ignore me as if my natural interest to communicate at such times was wrong and ugly and I feel like an old jar of marmalade left to mildew ... '

ACT ONE

(*These last words bring* CRISPIN *to a slow halt as the pain of* SIMONE's *letters reaches him through the last poignant image. He feels ashamed and retreats from her.*

TESSA *goes to* SIMONE *to comfort her.*)

SIMONE. Forgive me, Tessa. I couldn't keep it to myself all the time. I thought I could give him strength — that's not bad, is it?

TESSA. It's all right, don't go on. I don't mind.

SIMONE. You do, I know it. I can feel it in the way you touch me.

(TESSA *moves to be near* CRISPIN.)

Oh God, I feel so rejected, I can't bear it. There's such pain in this house, such pain.

(*The Friends are a tableau of misery and silence. They have known each other most of their lives.*)

ROLAND. I always think that while a *good* man sins or acts out some wretched piece of misery or offends his own gentleness, God turns away and doesn't look and leaves him alone to do it in private. That's a good world, that one, with a Good God. It consoles me, that. Doesn't make it easier to bear, but it's kinder.

Scene Three

Some hours later. About 2 a.m.

MANFRED *is reading at his desk and making more notes.* ROLAND *is sitting beside* ESTHER's *bed and reading to her from Djuna Barnes's* Nightwood. SIMONE *is by now drunk.* MACEY *sleeps in a chair.* CRISPIN *plays chess with himself.* TESSA *sits at his feet strumming a guitar.*

ROLAND. 'Nora had the face of all people who love the people — a face that would be evil when she found out that to love without criticism is to be betrayed. Nora robbed herself for everyone! incapable of giving herself warning, she was continually turning about to find herself diminished. Wandering people the world over found her profitable in that she could be sold for a price for ever, for she carried her betrayal money in her own pocket. Those who love everything are despised by everything, as those who love a city, in its profoundest sense, become the shame of that city.'

ESTHER. No more, Roland. Manfred, help me, I want to walk out into the room.

MANFRED. No, Ketzel, stay resting. We'll come to you if you want.

ROLAND. Let her walk.

ESTHER. I want to stretch and move.

ROLAND. Let her if she wants to.

ESTHER. You should be glad, shouldn't he, Roland?

ROLAND. She wants to step out and be alive. Come on, Kitten, ignore him.

(*Everyone rises to move things out of her way as* ROLAND *and* MANFRED *guide, like a queen, this pale and dying beauty to a stately chair.*

SIMONE *places a low, soft stool under her feet. They all seem to be play-acting an exaggeration of a relationship they each have with her — she is adored by them.*)

ESTHER. Come on, Manfred, you're dying to tell us what you've been reading about. We're all ready.

(MANFRED *picks up his papers and, with mock seriousness, begins to read from his notes as though recounting a thriller.*)*

MANFRED. You thought there were only three revolutions, didn't you? The French, the industrial and the Russian, eh? Well, you're wrong, listen to this, I've got more for you. This book tells that in 1600 a man called Gilbert, who

---

*It is of paramount importance that the actor makes as much sense of this precis as possible while at the same time clowning the story.

ACT ONE

was the personal physician to Queen Elizabeth the First, wrote a 'famous' book called *De Magnete* about an electroscope which turned out to be 'indispensable to the development of physical science'; and that in 1897 a man called Thompson discovered that electricity was made up of particles which he called electrons and this discovery had '*the* most profound effect on physical science'. Revolution number one. And then an American physicist called Millikan was able to *weigh* the mass of an electron as 1/1835th of the mass of a hydrogen atom and thus *show* that particles smaller than atoms existed. Revolution number two. Now, ten years after the discovery of the electron, a man called Rutherford, in revealing the nature of radioactivity, was able to break up radioactive materials into alpha, beta and gamma rays and in measuring the mass of an *alpha*-ray particle found it to be 7,000 times that of an electron and thus showed that the indestructibility of elemental atoms was a myth and so 'twentieth-century science was launched on its fateful journey into the restless world of the atom.' That was the third revolution. Now — it gets even more exciting — a man called Max Planck developed a theory called the quantum theory which said *radiant heat* was a discontinuous mass made up of particles and *not* smooth waves, and *that* was 'so revolutionary' that its implications were not fully appreciated until Einstein drew conclusions which themselves were 'revolutionary' because Einstein applied Planck's ideas with 'devastating results to the photo-electric effect and discovered that light itself *also* consisted of multitudes of individual pulses and not waves'. 'Physicists were incredulous'! Numbers four and five there. But that was nothing, because he then went on to the sixth revolution and evolved the theory of relativity which, as we all know, has the central principle that all natural phenomena are the same for an observer moving at one speed as they are for another observer moving at another speed, and *his* application of Planck's quantum theory to the photo-electric effect led to still more 'revolutions' in the theories of the nature of light and radiant energy. We'll say numbers seven, eight, nine, ten and eleven are lumped in that lot. Meanwhile, back in Denmark, a Dane called Niels Bohr applied the quantum theory to the behaviour of electrons inside atoms which led to *another* revolution—number twelve—this time in the theories of the structure of matter. However, Bohr was unable to find the spectra for complicated atoms and so he couldn't account for the behaviour of extra-nuclear electrons in any but the simplest of atoms. Now his failure became another man's challenge, and the next 'revolution', number thirteen, which was by a young German physicist in 1924 called Werner Heisenberg, who at the tender age of twenty-three set out to invent a mathematical theory which would account for the spectral lines which *could* be observed. But—also in 1924—unknown to Heisenberg who was courageously going forward—Louis de Broglie of Paris was going all the way back and putting forward the idea of a moving electron as a train of waves, and not, as Planck had said, a discontinuous mass of particles. And two years later an Austrian physicist called Erwin Schrödinger applied this idea to the behaviour of electrons inside the atom and showed that the permissible orbits were precisely those which contained a whole number of complete waves! Two revolutions there—numbers fourteen and fifteen. But—young Heisenberg was not satisfied with merely a mathematical description of the dual nature of the electron and so, in 1927, he introduced an extraordinary principle which is called the principle of uncertainty'—very wise!—which states this: 'that in the

ACT ONE

nature of things it is impossible to specify the exact position and the exact velocity of an electron at the same instant; the uncertainty in the position could be decreased only by increasing the uncertainty in the speed or vice-versa;' and guess what—the product of the two uncertainties turned out to be a simple multiple of Planck's constant! 'Of course, Heisenberg's uncertainty principle doesn't affect the behaviour of the world in the gross but its transformation of the fine detail from an exact and predictable pattern into a blur of probabilities was yet another major revolution in scientific thought.'

ESTHER. Wait a minute, wait a minute. Say that again—'but its transformation of the *fine* detail from an *exact* and *predictable* pattern into a *blur* of probabilities was yet another major *revolution* in scientific thought'?

MANFRED. Precisely.

CRISPIN. Really now.

ESTHER. Really now.

MANFRED. Revolution number sixteen. But the climax of the mathematical ideas of Planck, Heisenberg, de Broglie and Schrödinger came in a work which synthesized it all and was called quantum mechanics. It was written in 1930 by a Cambridge mathematician called P. A. M. Dirac and had the underlying philosophy that: 'Natural processes can never be described completely as happenings in space and time, because the observation of such processes is also one of the events which the natural process undergoes.' It was—this author says—'an epoch-making book'. Epoch-making! And have we read it? And all those revolutions—have we heard about them? And that was only up to 1930, there's another forty years to go! And my God! What shall we do?

ESTHER. You will grow bald and become blind and I have no patience with you any longer.

TESSA *(to a guitar)*.

Music © 1969 Wilfred Josephs

Freely - like an improvisation

We've bur-ied the win-ter mar-ried the spring, and now we have a time to pause and think a-gain and sing We've plant-ed seeds grant-ed birds their songs, now we have a time to rest and right a-gain those wrongs.

TOGETHER.

Chorus *(faster)*

If there's a heart in you, a part of you that can re-lent re-live for-get for-give then

(slower) *(faster)*

cov-er wounds I've gi-ven you for wounds are wounds and words are words and no a-mount of cry-ing cry-ing

(slower)

(slower) *(faster)*

cov-ers them or heals them_____ Live with them

(slowing down) *(slower)*

Live with them Live_____ with them.____

ACT ONE

TESSA. The leaves are turning,
The earth has turned,
And now there is a time for burning
Hates we left
Unburned.
The year's beginning,
Long nights will sow
Soft seeds for those softer days
The wrong ways
Must go.

TOGETHER. If there's a heart in you ...

ESTHER. Simone, stop drinking.
SIMONE. I'm not drunk. What does it matter?
MACEY (*who has slowly woken up during the song*). Jesus! what a head I've got. Why don't you all go to bed? What time is it? Two thirty in the morning, lunacy! Argh! My mouth's like starch washing day.
ESTHER. Simone, give Macey a long cool drink. Relax, Macey. It's the best time of night. I don't even feel tired.
MACEY. You just don't leave each other alone.
ESTHER. Feel this room, Macey. Quiet, friendly — it's a gentle room, this.
MACEY. Why didn't I go home?
ESTHER. Nothing can touch us here —
MACEY. You think not?
ESTHER. Isn't that so, Manfred? Manfred! What's he doing now?
MANFRED. The appeals, Ketzel — I forgot to sign the cheques.
MACEY. The what?
ESTHER. You didn't know, did you, Macey, that Manfred

forced us all to agree that one-third of our profits should go to help the third world?

MACEY. What profits, for God's sake? Am I in a madhouse or something?

ESTHER. Not charities, not cancer research or ex-prisoners, nothing marginal like that. Revolution, Macey: arms for South Africa, medical supplies for North Vietnam, funds for guerrillas in Latin America, books for Cuba.

CRISPIN. It should all be medical supplies.

SIMONE (*savagely*). Makes you feel more humanitarian, doesn't it?

CRISPIN (*imploring*). Simone!

ESTHER. The third world, Macey. We're all frightened of it. Our parents left us a heritage of colonial and racial bitterness and the third world hated them and is going to make us pay for it, and so we're all frightened.

MANFRED. Hatred is only an expediency for them, Ketzel.

ESTHER. Such a gentle person, my brother. Other people's need to hate makes such sense to him. *His* reasons for sending arms *now* is because they're oppressed *now*; mine are, the sooner it's done the sooner real men can take over from the rabble-rousers. Rabble-rousers frighten me, they're only rebels, not revolutionaries. My brother's a rebel, Macey, I—am a revolutionary. He talks about leaders of our time, I see a need for men who belong to the end of a long line of all time. He's obsessed with our responsibility to the twentieth century, I'm obsessed with our responsibility to an accumulation of twenty centuries of sensibility. My brother is a rebel because he hates the past, I'm a revolutionary because I see the past as too rich with human suffering and achievement to be dismissed. Women are natural revolutionaries, aren't they, Simone? Men are only ever rebels, their angers are negative, tiny. Like students, a kind of boyish energy. Do you know one

ACT ONE

of the reasons why I despise a capitalist society? Because it produces men who *enjoy* the violence of opposing it.

MACEY. Strange energies you all have. How can you concern yourselves with so much?

ESTHER. Macey thinks I'm teasing, Manfred; tell him it's only because I'm so wretchedly ill that I sound like teasing. Tell him. (*Closes her eyes.*)

(CRISPIN *begins to wander round the room, touching things, as though drugged.*)

SIMONE. Crispin! You look like a zombie.

CRISPIN. Don't shout at me, Simone. No retaliations now. I feel raw, lass. Harsh words is like burns. Can't take it. Peace, Simone, pax, pace, pace.

SIMONE. You're tender when you like, aren't you?

CRISPIN. Sssh. No little revenges, Simone; pace, pace, pace.

SIMONE (*mocking*). Pace, pace, pace!

(*Silence; out of which grows a contrapuntal duologue between* MANFRED *and* CRISPIN. MANFRED *whispers to* MACEY *while* CRISPIN *talks to the others.*)

CRISPIN. We've chosen good colours, gentle colours. Does that mean we're gentle, you reckon?

MANFRED (*coming down to confide in* MACEY). *I* know what I despise.

CRISPIN. It's that there's so much suffering in the world that I suddenly need other kinds of knowledge, to soothe it all out.

MANFRED. I know but I daren't say it.

CRISPIN. These colours soothe me, the touch of velvet, those paintings.

MANFRED. I've been feeling it for years, but I'd stutter if I tried.

CRISPIN. Is that wrong? To want to be soothed?

MANFRED. Even now, as I'm talking, I'm trying to bring myself to wrap sounds round those feelings. Perhaps, I think, my tongue will trip up, accidentally, in the middle of a sentence about something else. (*Pause*)

CRISPIN. Roland—

MANFRED. Hate them—

CRISPIN. Kiss me.

    (ROLAND *and* CRISPIN *kiss each other on the lips and remain clasped during* MANFRED's *next words.*)

MANFRED (*whispering almost*). The working class! Hate them! It's coming, Macey. Despise them! I can hear myself, it's coming. Hate them! The working class, my class, offend me. Their cowardly acquiescence, their rotten ordinariness—everything about them—hate them! There!

    (CRISPIN *breaks away from* ROLAND *to take* TESSA *in his arms, rocking her, cradling her.* ROLAND *lays his head in* ESTHER's *lap.*)

CRISPIN. That's what I want to do—I've just realized.

MANFRED (*still whispering*). Those endless dreary episodes of 'ordinary life' on television.

CRISPIN. I want to caress everything, touch people, comfort them, make them calm, tell them not to be worried, that it'll be all right.

MANFRED. And there sits the ordinary man, watching himself, pleased and familiar, not even spellbound, just dumbly recognizing.

CRISPIN. Have you listened to a car go round corners? Isn't that a violent noise?

MANFRED. 'Eh,' he says, 'that's me it is. Gladys, come and look, just like you and me and Jack and Gwen and Kate and bloody ordinary Sammy in the pub. No need to change then, is there? We're good enough to make telly about.'

CRISPIN. I can't bear violence any more, or the news about

ACT ONE

violence: car crashes, accidents by fire, famine, earthquake, war.

MANFRED. And then his children watch; and slowly they begin living a copy, not of their parents' real life, but the watered-down version other people have made of their parents' real life on the telly.

CRISPIN. I can't bear the violence of speech.

MANFRED. Isn't that extraordinary?

CRISPIN. Ugly people with violent voices, violent images on street corners, violent prejudices — it batters me.

MANFRED. But look what happens next, Macey.

CRISPIN. Me nerves — they're all frayed and battered.

MANFRED. Along comes a new generation of writers and they begin writing new episodes about the *children* — whose ordinariness has doubled because all they've had to look up to was the pale reflection of their parents which the last generation of writers put on the screen.

(SIMONE, *isolated, is drawn to sit by* CRISPIN *and* TESSA. CRISPIN *offers the comfort of his arms to her so that his strength is given to both women.*)

CRISPIN. Peace, I need peace.

MANFRED. And soon, Macey — you'll see, there'll be stories about their children and their children's children, and the characters on the screen will become more and more feeble —

CRISPIN. Peace and silence.

MANFRED. — and the more banal their utterances the more like real life it'll seem until one day the screen will just be blank, an electronic fog, and they'll sit there and accept it and say nothing.

CRISPIN. Peace, silence. Blessed peace and silence.

MANFRED. We're all poisoned by this hatred, aren't we?

CRISPIN. It'll be all right. Don't worry.

MANFRED. A real cancer, this one, growing from faint

beginnings, little suspicions, all those people we loved—
CRISPIN. I promise you—
MANFRED. Sad, like disappointed lovers, all that love, gangrenous, inside us.
CRISPIN. We must just be calm.
MANFRED. I try to ignore it, start afresh, find the world extraordinary—
CRISPIN. It's true—we must love one another, or die.
MANFRED. —but I've no energy, no appetites for new loves.
CRISPIN. Believe me.
MANFRED. Some men could, some men could stay perplexed and wondering all their life and still survive. All their life—
CRISPIN. It will—
MANFRED. —amazed!
CRISPIN. —everything will be all right.
MANFRED. Each moment—surprised!
CRISPIN. I promise you.
MANFRED. And finally—joyous! Joyous to be witness to it all. Lovely men they were, Macey, not sour and thorny like us, but eager, capable—splendid outrages. (*Pause*) Terrible!
CRISPIN. Peace—
MANFRED. Waste!
CRISPIN. —and silence.
MANFRED. That's what I really wanted to say.
CRISPIN. Blessed peace and silence.
MANFRED. We're too old to pretend.

(*Suddenly* MANFRED *stops speaking, his attention drawn by* ROLAND, *who is slowly rising away from* ESTHER *as though he has just discovered something dreadful. One by one they all turn to look at* ROLAND *and each of them knows—* ESTHER *is dead.*)

ACT TWO

Scene One

The same room. Some hours later.
The body of ESTHER *lies under some blankets.* ROLAND *has gathered a number of garments belonging to her and laid them at the foot of her bed. He sits, gazing at the body, holding a jumper to his face.*
SIMONE *enters in a dressing-gown.*
SIMONE. Roland?
ROLAND. She had an odour, a faint delicate odour.
SIMONE. Roland!
ROLAND. When I'd come into a room I'd know she was there. Here, this sheet, this blouse, a pullover — where her breasts were. If I hold it near me I can be reminded.
SIMONE. You ought to leave this room, Roland.
ROLAND. Not a perfume, nothing sweet and sickly, but the smell of movement, skin that had worked hard, to protect vulnerable parts.
SIMONE. Do you want me to sponge you?
ROLAND. Please. I think so.
   (SIMONE *undoes his shirt and pulls it down and slowly sponges.*)
   (*Referring to his self-immolation*) How crude that was. What a vulgar gesture. (*Pause*) You're not frightened of dying, are you?
SIMONE. No.
ROLAND. What will you do now?
SIMONE. I'd like to do just that: die, go away and die. Creep into the river or the stones on the street. (*Pause*) Give me a reason why not to, Roland. (*Silence*) You know what

defeats me? My capacity for nostalgia. I can project myself forward twenty years from now and feel myself regretting what I've not done today. That's what makes the present so oppressive; it's bad enough aching for the years gone by and suffering today's mess, but somehow I manage to suffer tomorrow's reproach also, before it comes. And it all defeats me. (*Pause*) Just walk out, away. Do it now. I'd get such peace. (*Pause*) Give me a reason why not, Roland.

ROLAND. You're drunk, Simone. Go back to bed. You've been drinking all night.

SIMONE. Never mind whether I've been drinking. Give me a reason why I shouldn't do it now, get up and walk away and never come back. You can't, can you?

ROLAND. I'm not the right person to ask.

SIMONE. You can't give me a reason, can you?

ROLAND. No, I can't. Please leave me alone now, Simone.
(*He takes up his simple Yoga sitting position and closes his eyes.*)

SIMONE (*rising*). You don't know what it's like to talk and not be heard; to offer and not be taken; to be full and not needed. There's not a creature needs me, not one single one. They'll use me, drink with me, tolerate my company, but not need—not really need me. And I feel so useless and rejected, so dismissed. You've never known that, have you? God's chosen ones you lot are, but not me. Look at my face. (*Looking into a long 'Gothic' mirror*) Long and Gothic you say, you like telling me that, flirting with the past. And my eyes, full of pleading. Who can look at them? Full of pleas and sighs and expectations—watery, dog-like; and long limbs—drooping over this chair, like a wet doll, awkward, embarrassing, waiting for crumbs; and they all know it, and they retreat. I don't blame them. Who can blame them? And I want to creep away, just

ACT TWO

pick myself up and go and not come back. I'd love that, I'd so love that.

(SIMONE *now regards* ROLAND *in his sitting position. Then, with great contempt:*)

It's all nonsense, Roland. Lie in green fields if you want peace, climb mountains or walk in forests if you want to meditate. You won't come to terms with death that way.

(*He ignores her; she watches a few seconds longer then leaves him. After she has gone he relaxes, opens his eyes, reached for a garment into which he buries his face, then crumbles, miserably, into the folds covering the dead woman.*)

Scene Two

Later. ROLAND *whimpering.*

ROLAND. Take me with you. I don't really want to go on. I'm so tired, Esther, and empty. Pick me up also, it must be so easy.

(*Silence.*

MACEY *enters. He's just emerged from trying to sleep, and is tucking his shirt into his trousers.*)

MACEY. I can't sleep in this house; you're whimpering all night and the others keep moving about. What the hell good do you think you're doing there, and those cuts all exposed? Put something over you, you bloody child, you.

(*He offers him a black pullover, which* ROLAND *ignores. Leaves him to agitatedly put on his tie in front of the mirror.*)

You're weird, all of you. And unnatural. Esther was the only healthy one of the lot of you. Just let the press get pictures of you all now. That'd be a scoop. 'The Trend-makers'! Huh! The habit of discontent was all your lot ever created. Making the young feel that the world

53

belonged only to them. Real little class terrorists you were, intimidating everyone over the age of twenty-five with your swinging this and your swinging that. You never thought you'd grow old or die. Even the politicians and the poets were frightened of you, you screamed so loudly about your squalid backgrounds. Here, let me help you. Look at you. They'll fester, those cuts. You must be racked with pain. And put a pullover on, it's cold.

(*He helps the pathetically struggling* ROLAND *to put on the black pullover, then wanders miserably round the room.*)

This room is festering. With gloom. Restless bloody house. (*Stops in front of* MANFRED's *model.*) Questions! Suddenly everyone's full of little heavyweight questions. 'Who do you hate? Who do you love?' 'Why are you a manager?' Who asks questions at my age? I know why I'm a manager, what good does it do me? (*Finally the atmosphere drawing an answer from him*) Because each morning I wake up knowing that I don't love the woman at my side, and haven't done so for the last fifteen years — That defeats me that does, that really does defeat me. No love — no appetites, for nothing. Even before the day begins I'm done. (*Pause*) But, I've managed. A good father taught me discipline so I managed. Why, I asked myself, why *exactly* did I resent her? Very important to know. She's not a bad woman, very good in fact, even wise — about simple things — loyal, sense of humour — everyone loves her — except me; so why? You know why? Because I had the capacity to grow and she didn't. She grew, true, but, one day she stopped and I went on. Simple! Not a reason for resentment, you'd say — such a strong emotion, resentment. True. But what I had to force myself to accept was that she was a reflection of *me*: I chose her. At one time in my life my entire capacity to love had focused on her. And I had to ask myself, 'Could

ACT TWO

I have been capable of such small needs?' So I resent her because she makes me despise myself. She reminds me, every day, that at one time in my life I'd wanted such small things. But the next discipline was really hard; you listening, Roland? Really hard! It was to avoid building up those little heavyweight philosophies about man and the world out of my own personal disappointments; to avoid confusing self-hatred with hatred of all men; to face the fact that though I'd failed, others hadn't. There! Two disciplines! Two honest confessions! But who's satisfied? No one is—are they? Because they're no good really, those little bits of honest confession. What am I supposed to do with them, tell me what?

(ROLAND *is trying to climb up alongside* ESTHER.)

What-are-you-doing-for-God's-sake? Get away from that body. Leave it alone!

(MACEY *in righteous anger pulls* ROLAND *violently to the floor, causing him great pain.*)

I'm sorry, son, I'm sorry.

ROLAND. No, no. It's good.

MACEY. Those cuts, I forgot those cuts.

ROLAND. Leave me, it's good I say.

MACEY. I just forgot them. I'm sorry.

ROLAND. It's good, I say. The pain, it's good, it's good, IT'S GOOD!

MACEY. You disgust me. (*Leaving*) If you imagine you can overcome death by creeping up on it like that you're mistaken. And not all your silly self-inflicted pain will help either. One day you're going to die and that's that.

ROLAND. There's no such thing as death.

MACEY. Idiot!

ROLAND. Death doesn't exist.

MACEY. Mumbo jumbo! Idiot! IDIOT!

(MACEY *leaves.* ROLAND *creeps back to the pile of*

THE FRIENDS

garments and again smells them, desperately trying to recapture the living ESTHER.)

Scene Three

An hour later.
ROLAND *still at the foot of the bed.* TESSA *is at his side, trying to draw him away.*

TESSA. Roland, come on, sleep, lovely.

ROLAND. I'm really frightened now, Tessa, of everything. I'm panicking. All those years gone and I don't like any of them and I'm panicking.

TESSA. You've given yourself too much pain, lad. Daft pain. And you're tired. Shall I make you a hot cup of tea? Without milk? Some lemon and lots of brandy in it? Will that be nice?

ROLAND. That tight brain I had, all wrapped up with confidence — it's fallen apart. Everything I love I don't feel for now. What do I do?

TESSA. Don't ask, Roland, please don't ask.

ROLAND. Panicking. I'm panicking. I can feel it, Tess. Terror and panic.

TESSA. Come away.

ROLAND. Where will it be? When I die, where will it be? How will it happen? Will I know I'm dying? Will I lie there knowing everything and knowing I can't stop it?

TESSA. You're not fair, Roland. It's not right, all this now.

ROLAND. Not even words. I can't find words; and words I find I don't want to use, and words I use I don't believe in. What do I do?

TESSA. Hush.

ACT TWO

ROLAND. Tell me, Tess. I've run down. Look. Stopped. That was my last word.

(*He has said it, but only after he has said it does he realize it must be true, for now he opens his mouth to say something and cannot. Real terror and panic show in his eyes now.*)

TESSA. Roland, stop it. You're forcing yourself. It's not honest. You can't stop talking. It's not possible. Say 'Tessa', say that. 'Tessa, Tessa, Tessa.' Scream then. ROLAND!

(ROLAND *releases a sad and desperate moan and pitches his face into* TESSA's *lap. She rocks him and laments.*)

Oh, oh, oh! My poor boy. It's so bewildering, isn't it? So wretched and bewildering. We're none of us what we thought we were. It's so late now. But you shouldn't panic, lovely. You shouldn't upset yourself. You upset us when you do that and we need each other now. Roland, we need each other so much. Roland? Roland?

(*She shakes him but he is in a catatonic state. Abruptly she rises.*)

Don't let his panic get you, Tessa, don't let it reach into you now.

(*She wanders around the room in a fever of distress — finally she reaches for her guitar and smashes it to pieces against the eighteenth-century chair.*)

Too late, Tess, too late.

(CRISPIN *comes to find what the noise is.*)

CRISPIN. Tessa!

TESSA. Oh, Crispin!

(*Relieved, she runs to clasp him and find comfort, but he cannot respond.*)

Aye, lad, too late.

(*She flees.* CRISPIN *collects the pieces of her guitar and places the ruins in a corner. Then he turns to* ROLAND.)

57

CRISPIN. Tha's frightened *now*, lad? Eh? Really frightened now. And I can't comfort thee, nor thee me, nor any of us t'other.

(ROLAND *shrinks and* CRISPIN *kneels and takes him in his arms and kisses his face as he would an unhappy child.*)

Aye, I'll tak thee in me arms and gi' thee kindness but there's nowt of comfort in me. I'm gone and messed up proper an' all. Shall I tell thee what I do, lad? Will that ease thy misery a bit? I'm so embarrassed and ashamed I can only tell thee in our dialect so's not to see the seriousness on it, so's it'll come out as a funny story. I sleep wi' owld ladies, me. I discovered one day they like me and they want me and I can gi' mesen to them. Owld passions I can drag from them, wi' me lips and me hands and a lot of gentleness. Tha canst not understand it, can tha? But it's like the glory of raising the dead to see red blood rise up in their faces and find their soft bones flutter wi' life. But they want to pay me and I takes the money and the pleasure on it turns to shame and disgust and I swear I'll not touch them again but I do. In the shop, they come and they look at me and they seem to know and their eyes plead and I go again. And there's shame and disgust and pleasure and it's all consumed me. Unnatural passions! They take out guts from a man. Aye, I knoa you can prettify it, give it justification, say the times they are a-changing. But times never made the soul, did they, lad? Eh? That's a constant that is, the soul, through all times, and what offends it today offends it tomorrow an' all. And I've destroyed mesen I have; offended and confused the soul, see? Denied mesen the right of saying owt to any man. (*Pause*) It's a good dialect, ours, ent it, Roland? We've noan on us got it still but it's a good, rich dialect from your smoky north. I think I'll keep it by me. Aye,

ACT TWO

tha's taken it badly, lad. And it's not ower yet. The morning'll bring its tempers, eh? Its snapping and snarling. We'll kick each other before t'day's through, that's for sure. Nay, there's nowt of comfort in me. (*Rocking, rocking. Fade.*)

Scene Four

Morning.

TESSA, MANFRED, CRISPIN, SIMONE, MACEY *and* ROLAND *are ranged in different corners of the room:* SIMONE *still in her dressing-gown;* ROLAND *as in the previous scene;* MACEY *his suit crumpled now. The rest are dressed in black.*
The three in black shift with heavy restlessness about the room not knowing what to do, each waiting for the other to speak. SIMONE *remains still.* ROLAND *is at the foot of the bed.*

TESSA. You look awful, Simone. Go away and dress.
SIMONE. Yes, Tessa.

(*She leaves. Silence*)

TESSA. Oh, I feel so old this year and not very wise.
MACEY. Well, and what are you going to do now?
TESSA. What's left worth the while to do, Macey?
MACEY. What a rag-bag of shabby doubts you lot are.
MANFRED. Don't fight.
MACEY. You think you've asked a question of such importance.
MANFRED. Please.
MACEY. But it's so thin, your question, so feeble and thin; such a puerile catechism to measure the world with.
MANFRED. Don't fight, please don't fight.

MACEY. And when are you going to bury her? Will it be a Jewish cemetery, Manfred?
(*Silence*)
TESSA (*to* CRISPIN). We've no children, that's what it is. We're barren, we're all barren; brought forth nothing, sterile. 'Barren and 'sterile': beautiful words, Macey. Too frightened to make babies, weren't we? They would bind us, couldn't have that, not us. Too beautiful we were, too important to be bound down. Dead lovelies, us. (*Pause*) Toys you made. For other people's kids. (*Moves to something we had not noticed before—a 'Crispin creation'.*) Lovely madness. The nearest *you* ever got to paternal instincts.

(SIMONE *returns. Somehow, with the exception of* ROLAND *and* MACEY, *the positions of each shift into a pattern where* SIMONE *is left isolated and the others seem ranged against her.* SIMONE *senses this, the others not.*)
SIMONE. So, the mistress is dead and I'm the first to go.
(*The others are caught off balance with this perception by* SIMONE *of what they are forced to realize was their subconscious feeling.*)
TESSA. What does that nonsense mean?
SIMONE. Oh, I don't know, a feeling I have.
TESSA. You have a knack of making people feel what they don't feel simply by suspecting them of feeling it.
CRISPIN. She's such a sensitive delicate soul.
SIMONE. It's not nice, what you're all doing now, not just.
CRISPIN. And she goes on and on misusing words. 'Nice'! Such an indifferent word: 'nice'.
SIMONE. But *why* are you all so hostile?
CRISPIN. Another word: 'hostile'!
SIMONE. I'll go then.

ACT TWO

TESSA. Oh stop it, Simone. Can't you understand for once?
SIMONE. And can't I be understood for once?
CRISPIN. She's complaining about being rejected now.
SIMONE. Talk to *me*, Crispin. I've got a name, I'm in the room.
CRISPIN. If I talk to her directly she'll think I'm in love with her.
SIMONE. You're very cruel, you, with your 'pace, pace'.
CRISPIN. Don't prompt me.
SIMONE. I don't understand, Macey.
MACEY. Nor me, none of it.
SIMONE. Suddenly, they're all turning on me.
TESSA. And stop whining.
SIMONE. I'm sorry about my voice, I can't help that, but it doesn't alter the meaning. You're miserable, all right, so am I. I haven't got any less feelings because I come from an upper-class family. We've got past that surely, Tessa?
TESSA. Well we haven't, so there! My father's a railwayman and yours is a company director and nothing can change that.
SIMONE (*hardly daring*). Except the fact that *you're* a company director.
MACEY. Ah ha! She has fight. That stings you, doesn't it. Tess!
SIMONE. Oh, Macey! It's all so unworthy.
TESSA. TAKE HER AWAY! Go, Simone, for God's sake go. Go and maybe by some miracle this room'll go with you. Out—get out, out—out—OUT!

(*Long pause*)

Oh, Simone. I'm sorry. You know we don't mean it. None of us. It's shock; Esther's dead and suddenly we're old and we're none of us what we thought we were and that's not easy now, is it? Don't cry, Simone. I've never been so cruel before, have I? (*Pause*) Oh dear mother, what's happened to me? It's stuck to me, this anger, I'm prisoner to it now, me. It used to be a joke for you all, I used to get angry to make you laugh, that was my role. But it's no laugh now. There's no getting rid of it, this croaking, I'm blotted with it now, for keeps. Oh dear mother, I wish I was a girl again.

(*Silence*)

MANFRED (*as though just discovering it*). There is about us all such a great poverty of intention. Such a great poverty of intention.

CRISPIN. Simone, I'm sorry if I—
SIMONE. I don't care for the sound of your voice just now, Crispin.
CRISPIN. I wanted to apologize, that's all; say I'm sorry. Peace—I want to make peace.
SIMONE. You only want to make peace because you've discovered a need for old women and you disgust yourself.
TESSA. SIMONE!
SIMONE. He won't give *us* his favours because he sells them.
TESSA. Shut up!
SIMONE. Can't be harsh to the world now, can you?
TESSA. Leave him alone.
SIMONE. Guilt's drained your energy away and you can't ask the world to be better than you are.
CRISPIN. I found this need.
SIMONE. Tenderness?
CRISPIN. Old women, lovely sad old women.
SIMONE. Ha! You need tenderness all right.
CRISPIN. I could make girls out of them.
TESSA. You rejected, sour bitch, you. What've you said?
CRISPIN. But it's true. How can you tell the world how to live when a passion like that takes you up?

ACT TWO

TESSA. Have pity on yourself, Crispin. There's no shame there.

SIMONE. I didn't say it to give him shame.

TESSA. Oh you've taken up a great responsibility now, Simone. A great weight you've taken now.

SIMONE (*softer*). I'll give you tenderness, Crispin. (*Both turn away.*) Macey, help me.

MACEY. How? Help you! Help you! How?

SIMONE. They started it, not me. I didn't want any bitterness.

MACEY. Bury the girl! What are you all standing around for?

SIMONE. They're disappointed and so they start resenting me.

MACEY. Is that all you've got the courage for? Bury the girl!

SIMONE. They think I'm silly, insignificant—a little bourgeois girl.

MACEY. At a time like this you turn on her. You need a thrashing, each one of you. Esther, bury Esther.

(*An attack is now gathering force from* SIMONE *and* MACEY.)

SIMONE. Look at them! Jumped-up downcast proles!

MACEY. They go around evolving their little panaceas and then get all depressed because their mums and dads didn't listen.

SIMONE. With their half-digested bits of self-taught education.

MACEY. The innocent charms don't work now, do they?

SIMONE. They've confused themselves.

MACEY. Why should your labouring fathers and tight-lipped mothers come to the shops anyway? What would that've solved?

SIMONE. They think I can't tell them anything.

CRISPIN. She's been drinking all night.

SIMONE. But I can. If they'd let me I'd tell them such things. I love them all so much, Macey; they've needed me and I've worked and loved them and I know what matters.

TESSA. What matters, Simone? You tell us.

(SIMONE *is caught off balance but struggles for a reply. Unfortunately her terror of them makes her inaudible, she cannot even look at them and uses* MACEY *to talk through.*)

SIMONE. Manfred shouldn't despise the working class.
TESSA. What was that?
SIMONE. And Crispin shouldn't be ashamed of his passion.
TESSA. I can't hear her, can you?
SIMONE. And Roland should stop hopping from one cult to another.
TESSA. What matters, Simone? We're waiting.
SIMONE. Justice.
TESSA. *What* did she say?
SIMONE (*still barely audible*). I said 'justice' — and the pursuit of happiness.
TESSA. But what's she mumbling for?
MACEY. She said 'justice and the pursuit of happiness', that's what she said.
TESSA (*incredulously*). But what's that got to do with anything at this moment?
MACEY. Well give her a chance, she knows what she means. Tell them, Simone.

(SIMONE *is petrified by now and continues mumbling into* MACEY *as though he must translate it to them. She is clumsy and touching and pathetic.*)

SIMONE. You see what I want to tell them is that order matters because —
TESSA. What's she saying now?
MACEY. She's saying order matters also, now quiet.
CRISPIN. 'Order'?
TESSA. It's becoming a nightmare.
MACEY. I bet that frightened you, didn't it?

ACT TWO

CRISPIN. Yes it did.

MACEY. Well you haven't earned the right to anarchy yet. You've created confusion and chaos and the habit of discontent and you haven't earned the right. Now, what do you want to say, Simone?

SIMONE. Tell them order is not uniformity or sameness. Tell them you can make order out of different things.

TESSA. For God's sake tell it to us, Simone. Mumbling away in that old granny's ear.

SIMONE. I'm just saying that order doesn't necessarily lead to uniformity or sameness.

TESSA. Yes—

SIMONE. And that you can make order out of different things.

TESSA. Yes—and so?

SIMONE. Well don't you see? There's a difference between the order that cripples and the order that liberates.

TESSA. Yes—

SIMONE. And that's what we're looking for, isn't it? The possibility of infinite variety? Isn't that—

CRISPIN. Noble?

SIMONE. Yes! Noble! So many blossomings. Noble! And what's more—there's room for failure when you've got order, and for weaknesses and—and—

CRISPIN. For everyman's fallibility?

SIMONE. Yes, Crispin, I don't mind being fed words, despite the manner in which they're offered. Everyman's fallibility.

CRISPIN. She's mad. She's been drinking all night and she's mad.

SIMONE. Oh, Crispin, isn't there anything in my madness touches you? Don't I deserve a little love for such loving madness?

MACEY. It's so terrible she wants to thrash your gloom from you?

SIMONE. Deny me that also?

MANFRED *(tenderly)*. Not now, Simone, not at this moment.

SIMONE. Yes, now, Manfred. Please let me go on, please.

MANFRED. It's all wrong to go on like this. I know you're distressed, you want to help, but it's all wrong.

TESSA. And irrelevant.

MACEY. Let her talk, Tessa.

TESSA. But she's talking about order and nobility and Esther's lying there dead and it's all irrelevant. Look at this room, look at the lovely order we've cluttered ourselves with. Dead and ancient riches, PERFECT!

(She kicks and kicks and finally throws over the eighteenth-century chair. SIMONE rushes to pick it up, lovingly.)

I can't bear this room any more. We've built too much of ourselves into it. Singing, plotting, loving—such a lot to be remembered, arrangements, smells, odd bargains—all that spent love and devotion—too rich, too too rich. And now we're trapped, hung up by it all. Bits and pieces of us all over the place.

SIMONE. You should love it.

TESSA. *Love* it?

SIMONE. Memory, the past, signs of human activity—you should cherish them—I adore this room.

CRISPIN. Millions starving and we've surrounded ourselves with thefts.

SIMONE. And would these poor bits and pieces feed starving millions? Is that the solution? More little gestures?

CRISPIN. Property is theft, Simone, don't you know that?

SIMONE. Nonsense!

MACEY. Nonsense!

SIMONE. Nonsense! Nonsense!

MACEY. The acquisition of property may be theft, but er—

ACT TWO

SIMONE. But the proprietorship of personal things? Little personal things? That's theft? Where's the logic in that? Look at this chair. (*Points to eighteenth-century chair.*) It's got to be somewhere, it can't be everywhere. Is the man who *wants* it and *has* it near him for most of the time a thief? Does wanting necessarily imply theft ?...

MACEY. It's not him wanting that's wrong, it's others not having.

SIMONE. After all, what does him 'wanting' that chair mean? It could mean that he's responding to beauty.

MACEY. That's bad? That's immoral?

SIMONE. Don't you see the silly confusions you've got yourselves into?

TESSA. The apple doesn't fall far from the tree, does it?

CRISPIN. She's returned to her class.

MACEY. Ah ha! Class! Class, class, class! And what a mess your lot made of that issue. I'll handle this one, Simone! The working class is deprived, you said, our society is unjust, 'stunted growth' you cried; 'promise unfulfilled'. And then—now listen to this lunacy, Simone—then, in the process of trying to redress the balance look what they did: they defended those very same stunted growths, called them working-class values and applauded them! And then they attacked bourgeois values as decadent. So tell me this, you idiots, you: if bourgeois values were only decadent and working-class values were only beautiful, then what were you complaining about in the first place? One minute you claim the need for revolution because inequality has left the people ignorant and the next minute you claim you want to do nothing but what the people want. But why should you want to do that which an ignorant people want? What kind of logic is that?

SIMONE (*swinging in on* MACEY's *excitement with confidence now*). That chair is beautiful because a craftsman exercised his craftsmanship on it. If an unjust society enabled one man to give another man the money to create a beautiful chair, does that make a chair a decadent work of craftsmanship?

MACEY. The trouble with them is, Simone, (*almost whispering to her*) they've taught the people to despise the wrong things and it's boomeranged right back at them. That's why their mums and dads ignored their shops.

SIMONE (*pulling him round to her, collaborators in mocking them*). You can't come to the people and claim that the things you like are superior to the things they like, because that will then place *you* in a class that you're asking *them* to overthrow.

MACEY. And you can't pause to argue subtle distinctions like that from a political rostrum—

SIMONE. Or in the middle of mountain battles—

MACEY. Or in the middle of mountain battles—

SIMONE. There's not enough time—

MACEY. The revolution's got to be done today—

SIMONE. To gain the people's full support they must pretend the people are aware and conscious of everything—

MACEY. Worthy to be listened to on all matters—

SIMONE. And so they find themselves involved in committing acts they despise in order to prove that the people are worthy to be listened to.

MACEY. On all matters.

SIMONE. And so you despise yourselves. For in this *you've* committed the most 'counter-revolutionary' act of all: in your haste to mobilize support you've given blessings and applause to the most bigoted, the most loud-mouthed, the most reactionary instincts in the people. (*Pause. No response. Tries again and then moves to switch on light over Esther's bed.*) But *she* was a revolutionary, a real woman and a real revolutionary. She wasn't obsessed with being respon-

ACT TWO

sible to the twentieth century. Twenty centuries of sensibility, the accumulation of *that*, that's what she felt responsible to. The past is too rich with human suffering and achievement to be dismissed. In the end there's such sweetness, she said, in hidden places, someone is always rising up, taking wing, and I want to be there. (*Pause. No response. Turning on them*) It's not me who's confused, because I've only ever spoken about what the working man *could* be and felt anger that he's abused for what he *is*. (*Pause. No response. Then with sad defiance*) Then I know this, *I* will neither wear cloth caps nor walk in rags nor dress in battledress to prove I share his cause; nor will I share his tastes and claim the values of his class to prove I stand for liberty and love and the sharing between all men of the good things this good earth and man's ingenuity can give. Now shoot me for that.

(*The others now seemed chastened and mellow, though more touched than convinced.*)

MACEY. They listened, Simone.

(*After a long silence:*)

MANFRED. Yes, Simone, we've listened. But that's not the half of it. Our mess is made of other things, like fears, pretensions and disappointments. It's not made of our confusion about who should own eighteenth-century chairs, it's made of—the silly things we've added to the world: easy achievements, ephemeral success. It's not because we've forgotten about injustices and the pursuit of happiness, it's because of little damages we've done to each other and a terrible sense of defeat and time passing and appetites fading and intellect softening. Our mess is not only made of Esther's dying, but the knowledge that this is a once and only life more than half over, and if you want to thrash the gloom from us then you'd have to give us back youth and the strength not to despise ourselves. Not all your haranguing us to order political priorities can clear up such a mess as that. It can't be ignored, that one, not that one.

SIMONE. THAT'S NOT GOOD ENOUGH! (*She runs to the dead Esther and throws back covers.*) She wanted to live.

ROLAND. LEAVE HER!

(ROLAND *snatches the body and hugs it to himself.*)

SIMONE (*dawning on her*). You've been wanting to do that all the time, haven't you? But you didn't dare, did you?

(*A strange scene begins; at first it seems hysterical, then macabre, but finally must become the natural actions of people trying to find their own way of both showing their love for the dead and trying to overcome their fear of death, or at least trying to come to terms with the knowledge of death.*

Everyone is electrified, uncertain, but sensing SIMONE *is about to do something outrageous. She watches them as though gauging how far she should go and then, cheekily rather than hysterically, raises a dead arm, making it 'wave' at the others.*)

She wanted to *live*.

(*She waits to see what effect it has on them.* ROLAND *is mesmerized, gripping Esther's body fearfully from behind. Now* SIMONE *makes it appear as though he is embracing her as she forces an arm to reach back and pull down* ROLAND'S *face to kiss the neck. The body seems to have life.*)

(*Whispering tenderly and reassuringly to* ROLAND) She wanted to live.

(*How are the others affected? She watches.* ROLAND *is slowly affected and makes the dead hand blow a kiss. At last a faint smile appears from each one and they shift in embarrassment and shyness, as though caught doing an improper act.*)

(*Realizing she's broken through*) She did! She wanted to live.

ACT TWO

(SIMONE, *encouraged, pushes them further by rushing to bring 'Esther's chair' to centre of room, and facing it towards the portrait of Lenin.* ROLAND *understands and carries the dead Esther to sit in the chair.* MANFRED *also understands and runs for a cushion to prop up her head. The understanding spreads as* TESSA *hurries to pick up a stool to lay for her feet.*

Now all stand back to look, awed at what they have done and what they see.

MANFRED *kneels and bends Esther's hand into a clenched-fist salute. The arm slowly falls.* CRISPIN *finds a book to place in her hands.*

Thus seated, the others are forced to accept the presence of the dead among them. Slowly they relax and one by one kiss her cheek, then—

MANFRED *returns to his model;* TESSA *and* CRISPIN *go to the bed to fold away the blankets;* ROLAND *sits by Esther as though guarding her.* SIMONE *begins to clear away coffee cups and dirty ashtrays.* MACEY *watches them a while, reaches for his jacket, half leaves, turns to smile at* ROLAND, *returns to kiss Esther, leaves—*

—and a slow, slow fading away.)